9 Intermediate to Late Intermediate Carol Arrangements for the Piano

DENNIS ALEXANDER

Christmas is a very special time of the year, and what better way to spend it than by sharing beautiful music with friends, family and loved ones. These special arrangements of some of the most popular holiday carols blend traditional harmonies with some contemporary sounds and are also very pianistic and musically rewarding. As Christmas is truly a time for sharing, the words are included so that friends and family may gather around the piano and enjoy the magic of making music together. May your Christmas be blessed with much happiness, beautiful music and good will.

Merry Christmas!

Dennis Alexander

for Darren

Silent Night

Silent night, holy night, All is calm, all is bright
Round yon Virgin mother and Child. Holy Infant so tender and mild,
Sleep in heavenly peace, Sleep in heavenly peace.

—*Joseph Mohr*

Melody by
Franz Grüber

Andante cantabile

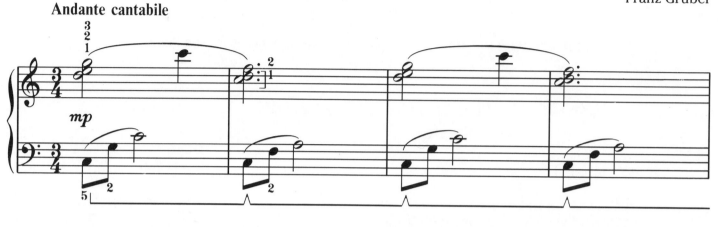

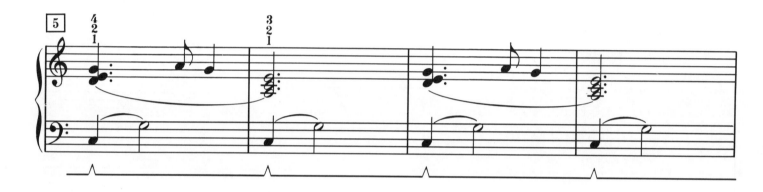

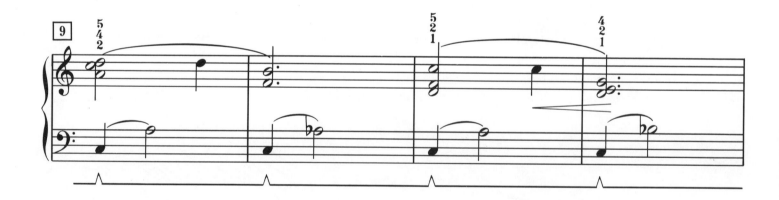

4

O Little Town of Bethlehem

O little town of Bethlehem, How still we see thee lie!
Above thy deep and dreamless sleep the silent stars go by;
Yet in thy dark streets shineth the everlasting Light:
The hopes and fears of all the years are met in thee tonight.
—*Phillips Brooks*

Melody by
Lewis H. Redner

Andante sostenuto

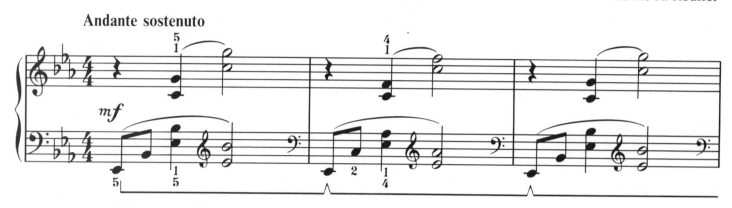

5

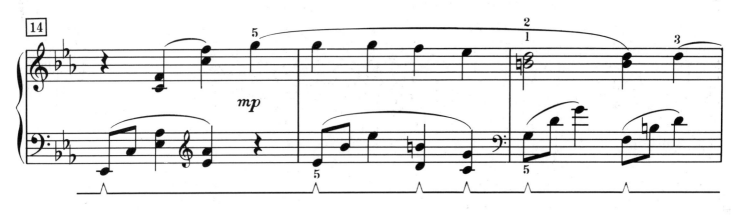

O Come, O Come, Emmanuel

O come, O come, Emmanuel, And ransom captive Israel,
That mourns in lonely exile here, Until the Son of God appear.
Rejoice! Rejoice! Emmanuel shall come to thee, O Israel!

13th Century Plain Song

I Saw Three Ships

I saw three ships a-sailing, a-sailing, a-sailing,
I saw three ships a-sailing, On Christmas day in the morning.

Traditional

Giocoso

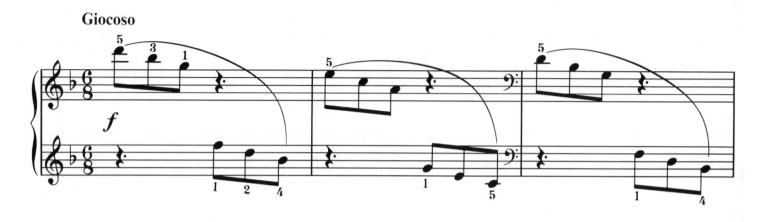

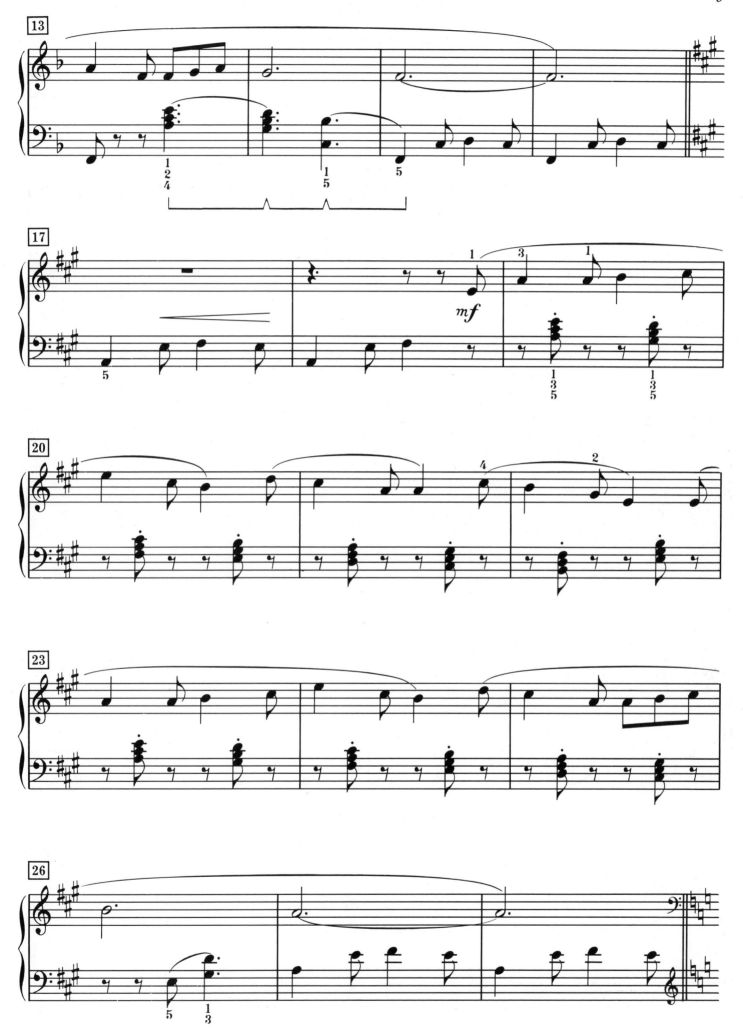

10

Still, Still, Still

Still, still, still, He sleeps this night so chill.
The Virgin's tender arms enfolding,
Warm and safe the Child are holding.
Still, still, still, He sleeps this night so chill.

Austrian

Up on the Housetop

Up on the housetop reindeer pause, Out jumps good old Santa Claus;
Down through the chimney with lots of toys, All for the little ones' Christmas joys.
Ho! Ho! Ho! Who wouldn't go; Ho! Ho! Ho! Who wouldn't go!
Up on the housetop, click, click, click,
Down through the chimney with good Saint Nick.

—Joseph H. Gilmore

B. R. Hanby

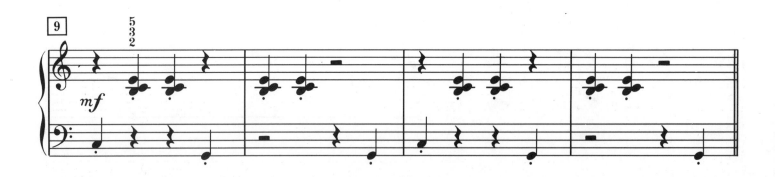

(both hands 1 octave higher 2nd time)

It Came Upon the Midnight Clear

It came upon the midnight clear, That glorious song of old,
From angels bending near the earth To touch their harps of gold:
"Peace on the earth, good will to men, From heav'n's all-gracious King."
The world in solemn stillness lay, To hear the angels sing.

—*Edmund H. Sears*

Melody by
Richard S. Willis

Moderato con moto

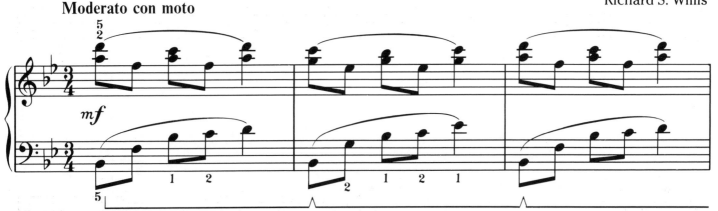

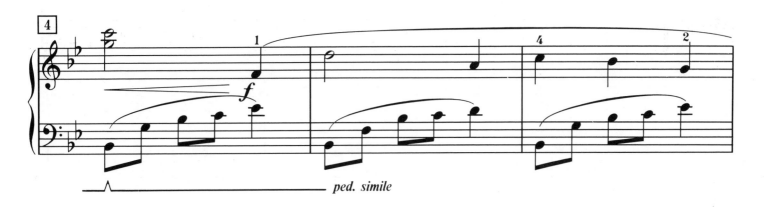

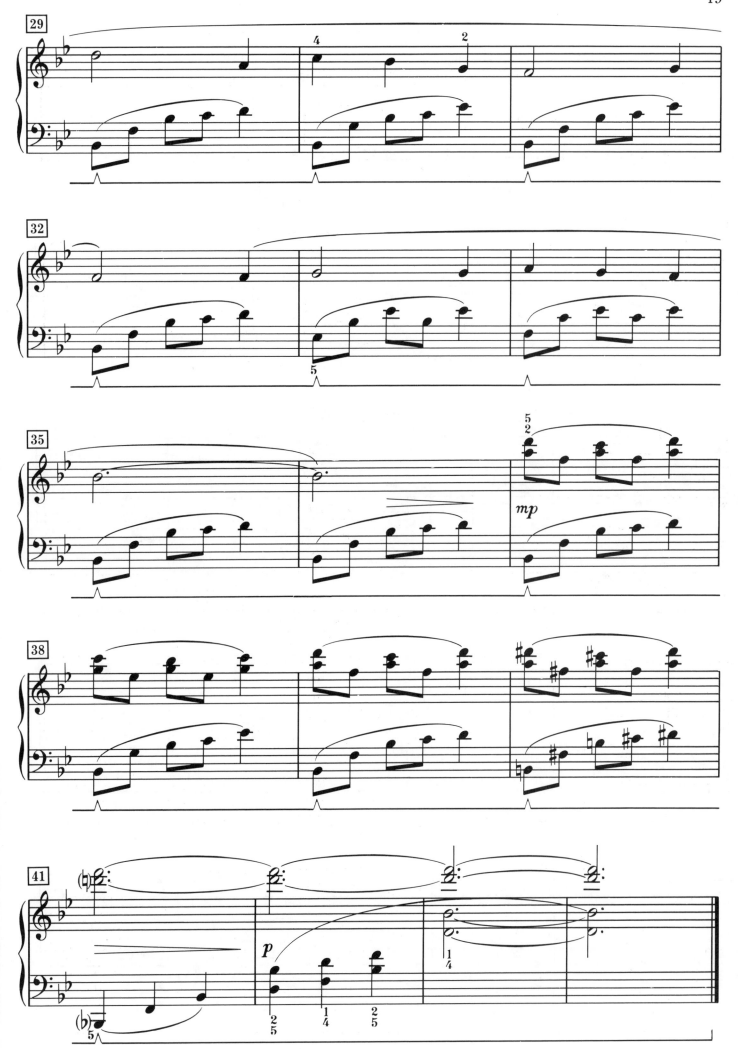

The First Noel

The first Noel the angel did say, Was to certain poor shepherds in fields as they lay;
In fields where they lay keeping their sheep, On a cold winter's night that was so deep:
Noel, Noel, Noel, Noel, Born is the King of Israel.

English Carol

We Wish You a Merry Christmas

We wish you a merry Christmas, We wish you a merry Christmas,
We wish you a merry Christmas and a happy New Year.
Good tidings we bring to you and your kin,
Good tidings for Christmas and a happy New Year.

English Carol

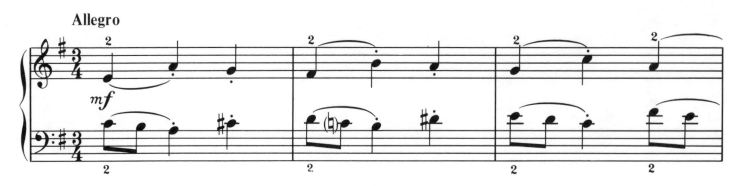

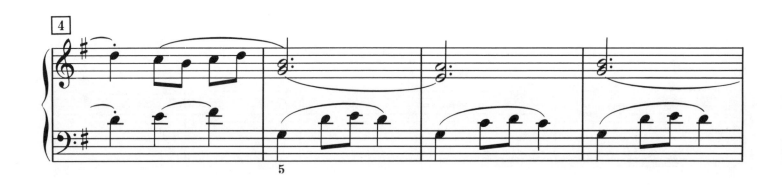